"Stacey Shoecraft offers ingenious alternatives to managing inattention in the classroom. Get the kids moving! Her techniques are inspired by her expertise and commitment to her students. This is a must read for all teachers and parents!"

~ Dr. Ken Coll, Psychiatrist

"Mrs. Shoecraft's infectious enthusiasm can be felt through the pages, and will motivate teachers eager to incorporate movement into their classrooms."

~ Tiffany Henderson, Assistant Principal,
Charles Pinckney Elementary

"What a great resource for teachers! I love this book. Stacey gives you everything you need to know in order to transform your class from 'sit and listen' to lets 'move and learn' like never before! This is an easy to understand reference for changing the way we learn, and has easy to implement strategies for anyone interested in improving the learning environment for students of all ages! Reading this book gives us an understanding of the relationship between movement and learning, and shows us why every student should be allowed the freedom to move and be active in the classroom. If you are not a teacher then buy one for your school — the students will thank you!

~ Ed Pinney, owner of KidsFit

"Having observed school districts in twenty-seven states, I have seen all levels of student engagement in many classrooms. What

Stacey Shoecraft has done is take student movement and engagement to an all new level. Stacey is definitely a model teacher."

~ *Paul Zientarski, Retired P.E. Department Chairman and Educational Consultant, Naperville Schools*

"Readers will be educated, entertained and enlightened after reading this wonderful book! Stacey creatively shares stories, ideas, suggestions and research that support the importance and tremendous benefits of learning through movement and 'brain breaks.' Written with humor and wisdom, Stacey explains with easy-to-follow directions and illustrations several quick activities and exercises which have allowed her students to more easily focus, retain information, regulate behavior and attention and increase academic performance."

~ *Marie Bosch, Assistant Media Specialist, Charles Pinckney Elementary*

"This is an excellent book filled with tips, strategies and activities for educators looking to incorporate movement in their classroom. I highly recommend this book to all teachers looking to increase student success."

~ *Bobby Sommers, ABL teacher*

"What an amazing resource! Mrs. Shoecraft has done so much to change the way we teach our students! She is an inspiration! I highly recommend this book! It will completely change your teaching style!"

~ *Cassie Connor, ABL teacher*

Teaching Through Movement

Setting Up Your Kinesthetic Classroom

Stacey Shoecraft

Chicken Dance Publishing

Distributed by Bublish, Inc.
www.bublish.com

Chicken Dance Publishing

ISBN-13: 978-1517152642

ISBN-10: 151715264X

Table of Contents

Introduction

It is sometimes the journey that takes the longest that is the sweetest in life. Sounds deep, doesn't it? However, it is true in my case. I consider myself to be a real life "Mulan". Remember her, the girl in the Disney movie who saves China from the Huns? Mulan's father told her not to worry about being like everyone else. His advice was, "The lotus blossom that blooms last, blooms best", or something like that. I haven't saved a nation from the Huns, but I feel that there is a mission out there worthy of a crusade. Problem is, I don't have an army like Mulan did. This is where YOU come in, I need your help! Don't let this stop you from reading this book; I think you picked it up for a reason.

 Disclaimer: In this book, I will be mentioning kinesthetic tables a lot. I do not work for the company that produces the tables, nor am I affiliated with them in any way except I use their product. That is important for you to know. My enthusiasm is genuine, and not a sales pitch to purchase anything. My purpose in writing this book is to teach, share, and encourage others. We CAN make a difference but often it is hard to figure out where to start. Therefore, I want to provide some help and insight from what I have experienced in the classroom.

 **Did you really just read this or did you skip the page? I never usually read the introductions, as I am thinking why bother? Now that I am writing one, I see that it is purposeful, so go back and read!

 P.S. I have the attention span of a gnat, I promise I will to try to keep these chapters relatively short. Hopefully, so short you could read them while in the bathroom. But don't do that because it would be gross!

P.P.S. Wash your hands before you leave.

CHAPTER ONE
The Early Years

Everyone has a story. I include mine only to let you know I have been "that student". From the age of six or seven, I played teacher and created materials for my cousins and friends, also known as my "students". As much as I loved playing school, I did have some issues with the one I attended. Not anything bad, just always having my name on the board for talking or daydreaming A LOT. All in all, I coasted by until puberty hit and things started to unravel in middle school. I was distracted by TV, phone, boys, and lint, anything that moved! My grades tumbled from honor roll to average and just coasting. You know the type, "Stacey is so smart, she really should work to her potential." My grades started to slip, slowly each year until I ended up graduating from high school with a "C" average and no longer thought of going to college to become a teacher. I didn't think I was smart enough, and I had that one teacher who reaffirmed it to me on a daily basis. He would always catch me daydreaming and chastise me in front of the class.

Fast forward ... now I am a parent with a young child in school. It was when my son was in first grade and his teacher said he might have a problem with paying attention. I was incensed and did not want to put my kid on medicine. Instead, I read a huge stack of books to try and fix the problem myself. You're not going to believe this; not only did I find out that yes, my son was probably ADD but ... so was I! My husband just shook his head when I told him my epiphany and reaffirmed he had known this, as he had suffered from my erratic behavior for some time. Poor guy! I eventually put my son (and myself on medicine) and it did help a lot. However, I have learned so much since then and think I was a little premature putting him on medicine. Why, do you ask? He only ate Slim Jims (beef jerky) and drank Capri Sun for his lunch during his fourth grade year and barely grew an inch because of his lack of appetite.

That, my friends, made me very sad and helped me to realize that we need to tackle teaching from every angle. Just last spring I saw our local newspaper with a sticker on it advertising, "One in five kids has ADD". Mind you, this was right after report cards were issued for the county. There was a number you could call to check to see if your child might have ADD too. I can envision this scenario: a parent looks at his or her child's report card and then wonders if it might help their struggling child to improve their grades. Am I against medicine? Yes and no, there are some children that might really benefit from taking it. I am not here to make a diagnosis, as I am not qualified as a doctor. What if we did something really crazy ... what if we changed our approach to teaching?

My goal with this book is to simply tell my story and what has worked for me. It is my hope the tips I provide will help you as you find your way. Changing the way teachers have taught for decades isn't easy. We are changing a mindset that students must sit still and be quiet. Change takes a lot of time and tons of patience too.

Chapter Two

It Has To Be the Dress!

I can still remember my first day as a substitute teacher. It was a fourth grade class in a nice, suburban school. I didn't even teach the whole day, just the last half. Things started out well enough until I saw the math. I know that I probably blanched inside as I saw geometry figures and terms I had not seen in sixteen years! I can remember feeling my ideal day slipping away from me, minute by minute. By the time it was over, I felt defeated. Being ever the optimist, I thought about what had gone wrong and reflected (as all good teachers do). I came to the conclusion that I probably needed to brush up on my math. Maybe I would even arrive earlier to look over the sub plans to ensure I really knew the material. Oh yeah, and one more thing, I was getting rid of the dress I was wearing because deep down, THAT was the problem. The dress was in the trash that night.

Moral of the story? Reflect, reflect, reflect. Think about what works, know your strengths as well as your students' needs. You need to consider what isn't working, and go shopping regularly; you're going to need it!

CHAPTER THREE

You Want Me To Do What?

I started my teaching career in a private school where all the children seemed to be homogeneous. No one had IEPs (Individualized Education Program) or 504 Plans (modifications and accommodations for students to perform along with their peers). After three years of teaching, I knew I needed to hone my skills because children aren't all the same, and I wanted to learn how to service all of them.

I went to a new school with children of all ranges. My first year I had a child, "Billy", who was never diagnosed with anything other than ADHD but had issues every year with his teachers and peers. I was asked to do certain exercises to help calm him. At the time I wondered how I would make this happen when I had so many other things to do in my day. Sound familiar?

How ironic that even though it was for one particular child, movement impacted the rest of the class as well. Not wanting to isolate Billy or make him feel singled out, I used the same exercises with all of my students. He seemed to be nonchalant about the whole thing, and it made me question if it was really worth the time to do. However, it wasn't long before other students asked if we would be having our movement moment, which made me realize how much they liked it too! Exercise gave the students the opportunity to move, and all kids need that, regardless if they have special needs or not.

It took a while before I connected the dots and realized there was a bigger benefit from incorporating movement in the classroom. This is purposeful movement, meaning it is dedicated to a particular purpose. In this case, movement is intentional so as to help the student reconnect and focus. Most adults can lose focus after about fifteen minutes; sometimes a little purposeful movement is all that is needed! I mentioned the attention span to emphasize students of ALL ages need movement breaks. How many times have you sat in a professional development class and struggled? Don't think purposeful movement is just for elementary students. In my experience, I have seen it used in middle and high school classes as well with very positive results. Former students of mine have returned to visit and were surprised when they saw their fifth grade classroom. They told me that even though they are in the higher grades, they wish they could have something like this in their classroom. It is really cool to watch them use the desks, see their eyes light up and begin smiling like Cheshire cats. Those poor students don't have recess or PE; their bodies are begging for a little movement!

We have seen this firsthand in a local high school here. One of the coolest things is the 83 percent drop in discipline referrals!

CHAPTER FOUR

I Don't Have Time To Do That!

I just mentioned how important it is to have purposeful movement in the classroom and yes, your brain understands it, but you have an agenda!

You don't think you have time in your day to stop to have a "brain blast" so you keep pushing forward. We all know educators have 5,000,000 standards to teach and not enough time in the day. I still have a problem with the concept of stopping, albeit briefly, which is why I have to remind myself that a brain blast is purposeful. I know what you're thinking, "No, really, you don't understand, I don't have TIME!" Yes, you do!

My concern in the past for stopping for a brain blast was loss of momentum. If I am driving home a point with my students and pause, then we will lose time for the lesson and I will run behind. Then I won't cover all the standards. Newsflash ... you are probably already behind because the students are "zoned out" and not receptive to learning.

In the previous chapter I told you the average adult has an attention span of about fifteen minutes. What I have discovered is movement allows the brain to refresh, or energize itself. Students are able to actually learn more because of this purposeful movement. However, when I "think" I really need to press on with a concept and don't allow them to move, it is a no-win situation. In the moment, I realize a pause of one to two minutes (or it can be less than one minute) buys more time on task for my students. I am not making this up, I promise I have seen it enough times to now know when to stop what I am doing and give students what they need.

Chapter Five
I am NOT a PE Teacher!

O r in other words: Why should I? You are probably thinking, "I don't know *how* to get the kids moving ... I am NOT a PE teacher!" Guess what—neither am I! That's not what this is all about. It's more of a control issue. Teachers like to have control, and many think if you get your students moving, you won't be able to rein them in to learn. I envision it to "cats on the ceiling"; how do you get them down? First and foremost, start small and state your expectations, just like everything else you do in the classroom. I always tell my students if they like the movement activities, they need to calm down and not act crazy after we are done. They understand it is purposeful movement, ah there's that word again! Because they like to move, my students are pretty compliant with my request. Although it sounds like a contradiction, allowing the students to move will actually help you with classroom management. Students need to be able to stretch and talk; this will allow them to do so in a positive way. Evidence proves referrals in schools decline when there is regular movement in the classroom. Exercise automatically releases a chemical in the brain called serotonin. To put it in everyday language: when you allow a student to move, they are in a better mood and more receptive to learning. It is like natural Prozac and Ritalin with none of the negative side effects. Look at the picture below of a brain that shows the difference! Another positive effect is the ability to focus more efficiently, hence how this is a natural Ritalin. A short-term result is the ability to focus for the next two to three hours, as well as improving long-term memory. The end result is a happy and focused child, which is what every teacher wants for his or her classroom.

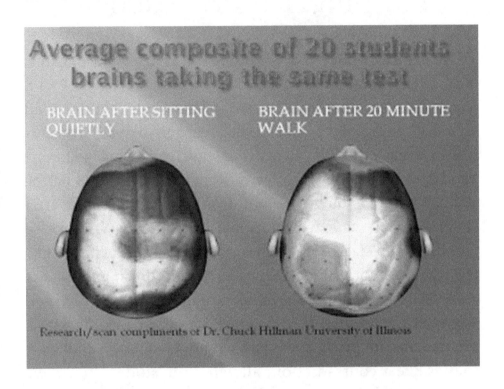

Average composite of 20 students brains taking the same test

BRAIN AFTER SITTING QUIETLY

BRAIN AFTER 20 MINUTE WALK

Research/scan compliments of Dr. Chuck Hillman University of Illinois

CHAPTER SIX
Boys Versus Girls?

As a teacher and a parent of two boys, the saddest thing was to hear boys say they don't like school. We hush them and tell them surely they must like something about it. Oh yeah, lunch, recess, and PE would be their favorite times of the school day. Of course, they are able to move! This progression starts in middle school and is clearly evident in high school. When I began researching this, I found that two thirds of boys graduate from high school. We are missing a third of those boys; that is more than a little alarming! I am usually an optimist, but there is more bad news. The graduation ratio of girls to boys from college is 60:40. I am not trying to make one sex more dominant than the other, but I do find it troubling we are leaving our boys behind.

What is the reason for the lag with our boys? Girls are more apt to have self-control and want to learn. They have more developed reasoning skills and understand that their effort in middle/high school helps determine their future. Sitting still is usually not as much of an issue for most girls, and they are more likely to pay attention. On the other hand, there are more cases of ADHD diagnoses for boys. The maturity level is not the same either; it is a well known fact girls mature faster than boys. Thus, boys don't see the big picture of why they need to sit still to learn. These qualities can be quite a challenge for them until they mature later in life. Therein lies the problem; boys (and girls) that are not allowed to move will eventually be left behind. If they don't conform to classroom "norms", then what are their chances to have future success? We have to THINK about how we teach our students to ensure we are engaging

ALL of them. The program No Child Left Behind is something we are all familiar with, yet we are leaving quite a few children behind when there is a solution right under our nose.

CHAPTER SEVEN
Baby Steps

For some teachers, they already have their students move in the classroom, so this is not a new concept. It is what they do on a regular basis. There is a "hum", similar to a white noise, and students move about while very much on task. That is awesome and yay for you!!

This is more for teachers who want their students in seats and quiet at all times. You might be surprised to know there are still many teachers afraid to get kids moving. Their thinking is, "What am I going to do once I get them moving and excited?" My advice would be to start slow, work within your comfort zone, and use a technique that works for you. When I first started incorporating movement in the classroom, it involved something simple like "Toss the Duck" (or whatever object you have) during a review session or to assess prior knowledge. No, not too original, but most things we use have been borrowed from someone else. The kids loved it because it involved throwing something, being out of their seat, and using movement. I use a stuffed duck and tell them the only rules are to not nail someone in the head, and my duck can't hit the ground. The reason why I like this is because it helps draw in kids who might otherwise sit there, especially my boys. Because who doesn't want to throw a duck around the classroom while answering questions? Rhetorical question, don't answer.

Once you have the students excited, you have to peel them off the ceiling. Not a problem! I sound like an infomercial, don't I? You too, can have a calm class for $19.99! I use the "Egg of Calmness" which is my only slightly original thought that I have ever had, really. Remember when you were a kid and your Uncle Bill (or whomever) would crack the pretend egg on your head? It felt really cool as it went slowly down the sides of your head. After I have my students move, I tell them to get their egg. How excited they are depends on the size of our pretend egg. Sometimes we have to get the ostrich-sized egg because I like to get my students pretty pumped up (I know that must come as a surprise). I tell them to "Crack their egg!" We use both hands and crack it on our heads. Then we let the "yolk" pretend to ooze down our head, on our shoulders, down our arms, down our bodies, and slide all the way to our feet. While we are still bent over, I tell them the directions. I talk calmly to them as we are doing this, and I explain and restate the activity to ensure they know what exactly is expected next. Once I have explained the transition, I tell them to come up slowly and be ready to move on to our next activity. The funny thing is after a while; we don't always have to go through all the steps. I sometimes just tell them to "Crack your egg!" they pretend to crack it on their head and quickly transition. It is a good way to bring them back without saying the same thing, and it is important to do it with them. I know I can get pretty excited, so it works for me too!

When I first started introducing kinesthetic tools to the classroom, I would bring in one object at a time. I always explained how it was used and would model it first, as well as have a student show how to use it as well. One thing the kids loved was the Sportime Duck Walker Agility Balance Boards (2.5 x 5 x 3.5 inch). You can find these to be inexpensive on Amazon and in magazines too. My students, especially my boys, would race to see who would get to use them first in the morning. My only stipulation was they had to be reading when they were using them. Nothing warms a teacher's heart more than seeing her boys read as they rock back and forth. I loved the duck walkers myself because it sort of reminded me of being on a skateboard. The only thing I didn't like was the sound on the tile floor, so I had the students use them on the carpet—problem solved!

Chapter Eight
Easy and Quick!

Who doesn't like a title like that? They both sound appealing! As I have said before, it is best to start small with baby steps because there is a higher probability for success. I want you to be successful, to be happy, and to help those kids move. However, many of you who read this are teachers and we know (I am including myself in this category) we have control issues, some more than others. We are afraid of the dream we have in the summer of our nightmare class, waking up in a cold sweat. This chapter will focus on how to implement quick brain blasts into your day. Just remember to state the movement, your expectations, and of course, carry your "Egg of Calmness" at all times!

Walk and Talk: One of my students' favorite things to do is to have five minutes of "Walk and Talk". We start our day by walking laps on our outside playground for five straight minutes right after the morning announcements before we jump into our learning. I keep an eye on the time and walk with my students. We talk about whatever they want to talk about while I walk the laps with them. Some of my boys like to run instead of walk and I am fine with that, as long as no one gets hurt. What can I say, if it gets their "ya-yas" out ... who am I to say no? After five minutes, we come together to form a circle, and I give them a little positive affirmation, or expectations, for the day as we breathe. Imagine me breathing like some exercise queen from the '80s and waving my arms up and down while talking to them. I say things like: "We are going to learn as much as we can today and a little more. We are going to be kind to one another. We are going to look for ways to brighten another person's day. Mrs. Murphy and I love being your teachers!" Then I finish it off with, "What kind of day are we going to have?" and they respond and tell me it is going to be fabulous! Our words are containers for power. What we say can directly have an impact on how we approach our day. At least that is my opinion, and I try to impart that on to my children (students ... same thing).

The mood has just been set for learning, and they all seem to be in pretty good moods. Although you may be thinking, that is five minutes and I don't HAVE five minutes; I think you might have that time. You can also adjust it to three minutes, use what works for you. I will tell you though this is a great opportunity for me to really talk to my students and see who may have come to school and had a bad morning. One of my students, Jimmy, was always in a terrible mood because of his little brother. He would hassle him sometimes on the bus, and it affected his entire day. Walking around and having the chance to talk to someone helped relieve the burden on his chest; it prepared him for learning that he probably would not have had otherwise. It is also great for classroom management! Think of the time we could have spent trying to redirect a student when they were off task. My students love the opportunity to be outside even for a small amount of time. It is like GOLD! Finally, we have our role as the teacher. Time is so precious in trying to deliver our "lesson" that truly getting to know our students as people is challenging. I look forward to our walks almost as much as the students because I can learn a little more about them and understand them as a person. In other words, we are connecting and I am able to check their emotional intelligence, EQ, to ensure they are ready to learn.

Basketball Hoop: This started because I had a Nerf basketball hoop and wanted to put some fun in my classroom. My students were in third grade and needed to be proficient with their newly acquired multiplication skills. I taught them a card game to practice their facts. As an additional enticement, I let the person who won the game make a shot. I should have realized they would love this part of the game, and I think it helped motivate them to learn their facts, definitely a win-win for me. After they played the game, students lined up to take one free shot. If they made the basket, I usually gave them a sticker or something else I had around the classroom. My fifth graders love it just as much as my third grade students I used to teach. Although I don't give out stickers, I have given out temporary tattoos as well as no homework passes—a student favorite! The funny thing is with the Nerf Basketball hoop, no offense to

tw.wonderteacher.com

Nerf, I felt like a "carnie". The kids would always take the shot but usually only one or two would actually make it, as the backboard wasn't that stable (insert evil laugh). This means you don't have to worry about going through a lot of stickers. Hey, that's how life is ... go for the shot anyway and have fun while you are doing it! You will notice in the picture below I have "upgraded" thanks to my kinesthetic godmother, Lindsay Beck. She always spoiled me with goodies for the classroom. This basketball hoop is a lot more stable, and the kids make more of the shots!

Does this work only for elementary? No way! I can see middle and high school kids loving this too! I also use the hoop to encourage participation. It seems as though some of my kids never want to participate. When I bring out the basketball, a lot more hands go up in the air. I also use the hoop to encourage students to become more organized. Once a week their morning job is to go through their binder and file all stray papers. If they see any papers they no longer need, they crumple it up and shoot. No worries, I have the recycling bin directly underneath the hoop!

Spinning Finger: Although I can usually of think of some way to get the students moving for a brain blast, sometimes I don't want the pressure. I would rather let the finger decide. Lindsay bought this for my classroom and the students LOVE it! She bought it online. It is called Educational Insights Spinzone Magnetic Whiteboard Spinners by Learning Resources. It is normally around $20, but you can find them cheaper on Amazon. You put the finger on your whiteboard and use expo markers to create a four square spinning chart. I put on mine "GoNoodle" (I will explain that later), chair yoga, squats, or teacher's choice. When students are feeling tired, I ask them to spin the finger and it decides for us. (I should do that for dinnertime! It would make it much more exciting!) The students love it, and you can tell which activity certain students love most. One of the great things about the finger is you can make changes and try out new brain blasts. It is a way to keep things "fresh". We have also used the spinner during a math lesson on probability. After a while we noticed the amount of times it would land on certain activities and started to chart it.

www.wonderteacher.com

After a while of looking at it and making observations, the students came to the conclusion certain events would be picked because the weight on the finger wasn't evenly distributed. It is a very slight variance, but my sharp students picked up on that. They then came to the conclusion gravity and the pull of the mass of the finger altered the probability of certain events being chosen. That was a fun, teachable moment that happened because of allowing movement in the classroom.

Resistance Bands: I would have never thought to get these on my own but a professor, Dr. Karen Smail from the College of

Charleston, suggested I add them in my classroom. I like the bands because they are different and yet another way to change

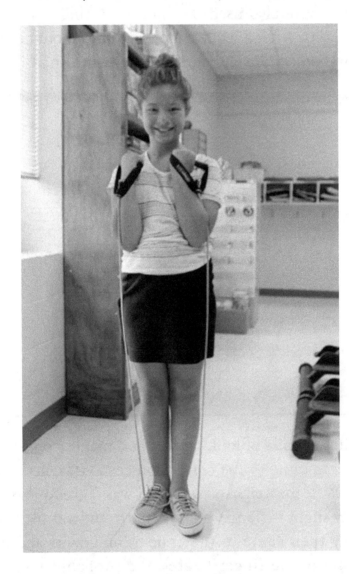

things up. Boys (and girls) seem to gravitate towards them for the same reason, and the bands are especially appealing to students who do not like to dance. We use these resistance bands for a quick brain blast lasting one minute, or less! You can purchase the bands at a local store, Amazon, or I think the best deal I have seen is on eBay: five feet Thera-Band, latex free, special heavy resistance exercise bands for around $5 and free shipping. Holy cow, what a deal! I just found this for you; I promise I am receiving no royalties from the company! The best part is you can cut them, so everyone in your class has one to use.

Wobble Cushion: The ones I purchased have a textured, knobby side, and I have been told by my resource teachers that is sensory input which is good for autistic students. Since I am working with a professor, she is the one who told me all about them. As a result, I was able to get them through a grant. Otherwise, you can purchase a small amount and have the students take turns. They aren't terribly expensive, (around $12) yet we know how much teachers pay for all the things in their classrooms. The wobble cushion is an ideal tool for improving balance, coordination, and flexibility. The cushion requires the student to use more muscles to stay balanced. It is good for active sitting, as opposed to passive sitting. I love them because they are portable. We take our cushions to assemblies, when students are expected to sit on the hard gym floor. In my classroom students put the cushions in their seats and we sometimes use them as quick brain blasts.

For teachers who like to bring their students to the carpet, this is an easy way for kids to have their own space and yet allow for a little movement. It really is hard for some to just sit still! The surprising thing I found out was how much I loved them! I got rid of my "teacher chair" and put one on a regular student chair. I tell the kids I am working on my abs, joking that I will be able to shred cheese on my stomach by summer. You really can feel it working. So if it works for a grown woman, it could definitely be used in middle and high school. Students would welcome a softer seat that allows them to move. They are not as "grown" as we think they are. Maybe it might even make them enjoy school a little more. Worse things could happen.

Running Laps: I don't know about you but I do not have enough time in the day, ever! I have good intentions, but it seems as though I don't work out as often as I should. Running laps happened by accident, and it is so good on so many levels! Around March, my students started acted CRAZY and were driving me CRAZY ... short drive. I decided they need more than a Walk and Talk; they needed to run because they had way too much energy for me. We went outside, and I told them we were only out there for our usual five minutes in the morning. The first day, I told them they had to run the first half, and they could walk the second half of the loop in our parking lot. Some of my students are a little out of shape, so I suggested skipping too. They LOVED it! The next day I told them the amount of laps they did would count for their Class Dojo (a free online classroom management tool and app) and they would earn the same amount of points equal to what they ran. Here is the link for Class Dojo: dojo.com. Talk about upping the ante; they were going at breakneck speed! The funny thing is, my classroom calmed down a lot. I was in heaven and curious to see how we could tweak this. One of my classes had more than ten ADHD students in it, some medicated and some not. I decided to take them out for a quick three to five minute jaunt before we started our math lesson, and it was so successful I continued to do it for the rest of the school year. This helped them to calm down and focus on their learning. I believe their bodies were looking for a way to release the potential, or stored energy; sometimes we all need a big burst. During this endeavor, I realized I should do more than my weekend warrior of running and biking, as it just wasn't enough. After a few days of walking while they ran, I decided I should lead by example. For me, running is great because I am wide-awake, energized, and have multi-tasked ... at least that little bit of running is better than no running. What can I say, I am a work in progress.

Bosu Ball: This can be used as a center or to use at the Smart-board. Personally, I like it as a center more. I am a big fan of KenKen, a Korean math puzzle similar to Sudoku, and in this center the students are solving KenKen while standing on the Bosu Ball. The sky is the limit in how you choose to use this piece of equipment.

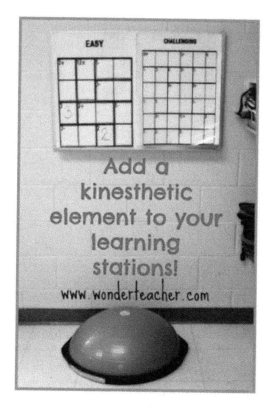

CHAPTER NINE

All at YOUR Fingertips

When Al Gore invented the Internet, who knew how important it would be to the classroom! Seriously, besides the few things I have told you about, the Internet has been one of my BEST resources for incorporating brain blasts into our daily routine.

Chad Triolet: While searching the Internet, I found Chad Triolet's YouTube page with choreographed dance videos. Chad is a Physical Educator for the Chesapeake Public School System in Virginia. My students loved him because he was easy to follow and gave tutorials before the dances. As a result, they didn't feel as awkward if they didn't know it. I think it actually made them more confident in front of their peers. They liked the Thriller dance so much, we decided to make our own and then showed it to the rest of the school on the news, right before Halloween. It was Spooktacular! These brain blasts take about two to four minutes, and I usually use them in the morning to get the happy vibes flowing. Really, I am getting them ready to learn and they don't even know it. I am so sneaky.

Deskercises with Dave Spurlock: Little did I know what a HUGE impact Dave Spurlock would make on me when I first met him. He is a longtime coach and does the job of three men, or more. One of the things Dave taught me was how to use desks to your advantage. He showed me a website, videos created with the intention of purposeful movement (http://academicdepartments.musc.edu/leanteam/deskercises/).

He refocuses the students with very quick cardio activities and some yoga too. I love this and use it with my spinning finger as a choice for a brain blast.

GoNoodle: A website that has been my go-to for over a year now. I appreciate how they are always trying to change and keep things fresh. It is like a treat within a treat! They periodically have sent us stickers and pencils, and the students love to earn points by participating. We have spent more than twenty-two hours (I kid you not) in less than one school year by completing these brain blasts. When I say we, I mean my buddy and team teacher, Laura Murphy, so don't sweat it ... we are actually learning. It helps build the classroom family, as they see the points we accrue and that we are doing this together. Laura loves Zumba the best, and it has about thirteen different songs on it. Definitely gets the blood pumping! I have several I like, so it is hard to choose. I like Koo Koo Kanga Roo because of the silly and weird factor. If you have a student who doesn't want to dance, this is the one to do! I showed this to a class of five year olds, and they were able to mimic the moves. Their favorite was the Dinosaur Dance, not a big surprise! Besides Zumba and Koo Koo Kanga Roo, they also have Indoor Recess, a nice alternative to the caveman favorite of "Heads Up-Seven Up!" I also like Maximo, a talking monkey who teaches yoga. I really feel the stretches afterwards and love him. He is hilarious. The kids love him too! Something else I am starting to use is Brainercise. It looks awesome because it helps students cross the midline while sending neurons flying down different paths. We truly do need to reprogram our brain's thinking patterns. The videos are about one minute and forty-five seconds or less, which is perfect for a quick stretch. Finally, my other favorite on that site is the Run with Us. They have Olympic athletes who give positive messages to students prior to the event. It is hilarious to watch the kids running and pretending to jump the hurdles. I like it because it wears them out and entertains me, a win-win for everyone. Big question: what ages would this be appropriate for? I definitely see this as elementary for most, but I can also envision middle and high school kids doing the sports or even the other ones, just for a break. Will they do it the first day? Probably not. The best way to get kids involved is to do it with them, regardless of their age.

CHAPTER TEN
What Other Teachers Do

Lindsay Beck, the woman who first exposed me to all of this, was kind enough to share her expertise as well. These are the guidelines she has for using movement concepts to FULLY engage the brain:

1. Establish high expectations.
2. Model each movement station.
3. Use daily repetition.
4. Ensure student success prior to moving on.
5. Practice doesn't make perfect.
6. Practice makes PERMANENT.
7. Have consequences for moving out of control.

Lindsay mentioned an import aspect I need to focus on more when telling others about the importance of kinesthetic learning. Practice makes permanent. Many times students memorize something only to forget it later. By practicing repeatedly, we are creating a path in our brain to help us recall and retrieve the information. It will help us retain this as a long-term memory. I think that is pretty cool!

Instead of describing and having you try to "picture" this in your mind, I will show you instead. Lindsay reminded me they weren't all her ideas but a conglomeration of many. One of the lessons we first learned was to beg, borrow, and steal. I am not stealing (just sharing).

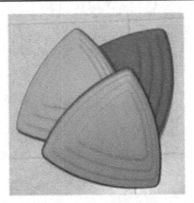

Stepping Stones

Commutative Property

Obviously, "Stepping Stones" can be for several grade levels, and it makes me think I need these too!

Spelling Words

Besides using these for spelling words, I also thought of it for vocabulary words too. Don't think this is just for younger kids either, I know older kids would LOVE to get out of their seat as well.

Using this high-energy activity, "Stomp and Catch", could also be used for multiples when teaching multiplication. Any other ideas come to mind?

Stomp' N Catch

Count by 5's, 10's, 100's

The cones could be used when discussing sequence of events, vocabulary, or answering comprehension questions.

Cones

Over

Although I use balance discs (I call them wobble cushions) for my students' seats and on the carpet, they are also a useful tool for this activity. As mentioned in Chapter Eight, I also have my students bring them to assemblies so they can pay attention; it is HARD sitting on a gymnasium floor! You could use this at any grade level. A couple of examples for ways to use the wobble cushions that came to mind were identifying the Periodic Table of Elements or identifying parts of a plant cell ... to name a few!

Tennis Racket

Skip Counting

I love this because it makes the ordinary, extraordinary! I can visualize students enjoying the variety of ways to learn. The BEST part is that it isn't going to be the normal rote memorization and "data dump". Since movement is involved, learning becomes permanent, not temporary.

Fit Deck

Spelling or Vocabulary Words

Movement, in any form is a beautiful thing. One of my favorite teachers is quite innovative in everything she does. I am in awe of how she seems to do everything so effortlessly. Stephanie Cordray was the first teacher in our school to use yoga balls, an entire class set of them! I was worried they would roll everywhere; I know you were thinking the same thing but they don't. Of course she came up with a solution, and her room is as tidy as ever! She has the students place them in Frisbees so they don't roll away.

After Stephanie acclimated the students to the balls, she purchased wobble seats for her kidney table. They look like the wobble cushions I mentioned earlier, except they are similar to a chair. I researched them and found out some interesting information. The chair strengthens core muscles, promotes proper posture, and is said to be good for students with ADD and ADHD. They are about $50 each, and I believe she used the stipend we receive at the beginning of the year to pay for this. Another idea would be to go on the website Donors Choose to help you pay for them. Just to give you a visual, I found this one on SharingKindergarten.com.

Another friend of mine loves to use centers and hers are very kinesthetic! Although Cassie McKay teaches high school, she still believes in the importance of movement. She and many other PE teachers will tell you it is not just movement; it is purposeful movement, as it rewires the brain and prepares it for learning. One of her activities includes having the students use the plank position (or use a yoga ball) as they are using matching cards on the floor.

One of her "go-to tools" is to use ladders (a real ladder or you can use painters tape) for students to step across as they answer questions. Balance seems to be a focus, as is evident with the rubber half domes (J-Fit Balance Pods). She has the student stand on one foot while solving a math problem. Another way she uses them is to spread them out to create a stepping path for students while they complete a task.

Chapter Eleven

And the Survey Says...

If you want to know what the truth is, go to the source, and that is exactly what I did. My goal is to help other educators, myself included, understand students' perspective and best serve the students' needs. Isn't that why we are all teachers in the first place?

With the promise of anonymity, I interviewed the entire fifth-grade class at our very large school. Nearly 320 students responded to my questions. My first question was, "How often do you get in trouble at school?" 23.9 percent (or 76 students) replied they never got in trouble. Secretly, don't you wish they were all in one class? It sounds good in theory, but I wonder if it would be too boring without the cheeky kids, you know the ones full of sparkling personalities! 51.3 percent (or 163 students) said they hardly ever get in trouble. You are probably thinking I am making this up, I am not. We really do have a marvelous bunch of students and for that I am very thankful. 22.2 percent (or 70 students) stated they sometimes got into trouble. In the last group 2.8 percent (or 9 students) confessed to having been in trouble more times than they would like to admit.

Here are the reasons students gave as to why they got into trouble:

- Talking.
- Not being focused and playing with stuff.
- Talking when I am not supposed to, not paying attention.
- Talking in class.
- Messing around.
- I sometimes forget my homework and am not too

organized. I will get in trouble for not being on task or talking when I'm not supposed to.

- I get in trouble for doing things like doodling; I constantly have to be doing something!
- Mostly talking considering class can get a bit, well, boring.
- I only get in trouble when I occasionally forget to do my homework, or turn something in. Sometimes I get caught doodling something, but doodling helps me think!
- Not paying attention in class and talking to friends.

If the students responded "yes" to getting into trouble, they were then asked if sitting too long might have been the reason. Seven out of the nine students who responded they were in trouble more times than they would like to admit, stated boredom, sitting too long, and inability to focus as the reason for interrupting classroom instruction.

You may have wondered why I asked that particular question. I have a theory of time spent in "active play" versus passive play in front of a screen or doing things that do not require the use of the larger muscles, such as drawing or reading. If children have an opportunity to expend their energy, I believe they will have a calmer state of being. Think of a roller coaster when it goes down a hill and hits full speed. It is letting go of all of the stored energy. Children are the same way; they need to get rid of some of that stored energy! Another MAJOR reason is balance. When I first heard about how important balance is in regard to focus, I thought to myself, "Yeah, right, I don't believe it." The more I observed my athletic students; I began to see the correlation. The students who are clumsy are less likely to play sports requiring physical dexterity. These same students come into the classroom with potential (stored) energy and have a need to release it. It then becomes our job to help students find a positive way to expend their energy. They need to know that as teachers we are on their side and support them. These struggling students already have a self-esteem issue and feel they can't keep up with the jocks in the class. Not only are they struggling on the baseball field because of lack of balance, now they struggle in the classroom because they can't focus. For the sake of sounding trite, the struggle is real, and we lose these students in the process. I AM that student who was clumsy, liked to draw, read a lot, and didn't focus. School became a struggle. You feel like you aren't smart enough. Yet, the opposite is true, these students are smart; we just need a new way to reach them.

The next question I asked was, "What is the hardest part of sitting while you are learning?"

- You can't move while you're sitting and I can't do anything without moving.
- Just sitting there kind of makes me want to go to sleep. I will always tap my finger on the desk or cross my legs just to do something.
- That I can't move and I am just sitting there.
- Not moving.
- The hardest part is sitting.
- Not moving around can really bore me to almost sleeping. I have nothing to do with my legs because I am used to moving my legs around.
- I need to get my energy out of me.
- DOING NOTHING.
- The hardest part of sitting is when your butt starts

hurting and you feel like you really want to stand up even during a test.

- Sometimes after I sit in my seat for a long time, I really want to get up. I feel like I need to move around. Then it becomes hard to focus on what we're doing in class.
- I get bored and tired and am not engaged in my learning.
- I can't stop moving like one time we were doing a math sheet and I was standing and moving my feet but still working and I got in trouble. Another thing is if I do sit, I still move my feet and I tap them on the ground. My teacher gets mad when I do that, so I get in trouble for that a bunch too.
- Leaning back, I love leaning back in my chair, but we're not allowed to do that.
- Doing nothing with nothing else to do, sort of like a jail.

Reading their responses is so sad! I could go on, but they are all pretty much the same. Kids are begging for the ability to move, and it would benefit them and us. My students are a testimony to this thought and have told me what it does for them. Blake told me, "I get more fit. I am able to calm myself, especially if I am stressed." Calvin told me the ability to move helps him to focus.

Another one of my students, Edward, reminds me of a small bouncy ball. His reply when asked was, "You are allowed to get rid of energy and get ready for class." This is true and so funny to see, as I will sometimes look over at him and he is moving a mile a minute. Yet, he isn't getting in trouble for it, and it helps him to reconnect in class. Finally, another sweet girl of mine has a myriad of issues to deal with, including Autism, and she has told me it helps her in two different ways, her mind and body.

Teachers and administrators, are you hearing this? What are some options? Here are some of the activities and things kids told me they like doing with regard to classroom movement:

- PE was a huge favorite of theirs. I do have to brag on our awesome PE staff. They asked what we were doing in science and incorporated learning about Newton's Three Laws of Motion while the students were playing a game. Awesome!!
- Active Brains is another big favorite. It is a special area, just like music and art. Our Active Brains teacher, Bobby Sommers, teaches them a mini-lesson (a concept they have already learned in class from us) and then they go through a circuit of different active activities. I love it because it helps reinforce what they have learned with me.
- Yoga balls are a big hit with the students.
- Perhaps it is because you really have to focus on using them properly, and they allow for so much movement or maybe because they are just fun.
- Wobble seats and duck walkers are another of their favorites and something I have previously mentioned.
- Drama is another big favorite of students. If your school doesn't have a drama teacher, that doesn't mean you can't have it. Why not have a Reader's Theater? There are numerous books for Reader's Theater, and it is amazing how much they learn by performing.
- Movement tables were also mentioned a lot, and you know that warmed my heart! I'm so glad to see it does make school a more enjoyable place for students to learn.

CHAPTER TWELVE
Nice! But Can You PROVE It?

Many of you who are reading this are already familiar with the awesome book by Dr. John J. Ratey, *Spark: The Revolutionary New Science of Exercise and the Brain*. As a result, you know movement DOES make a difference. The results are in and yes, there is proof. That isn't what you are asking though; I think you want to know if I have seen proof.

Although we are still researching the classroom and each year looking at a different independent variable, undeniably each year we return to the same positive affirmations. Last year the College of Charleston, under the direction of Dr. Karen Smail, focused on heart rate, balance, and time on task. The results of the test are as follows: boys were more passively engaged while girls were more actively engaged. Heart rate data was collected using Mio heart rate monitors. Heart rate fluctuations seen in students showed that kinesthetic desks elevated heart rates when engaged in learning. No significant changes were found in resting heart rates. Balance was measured using the modified stork stand test. Improvements were found in both eyes closed conditions; however, results were not statistically significant. Significant improvements ($p=0.04$) were observed in the eyes open condition with left leg standing. What does this all mean? The final outcomes were 30 percent of boys actively used the kinesthetic tables, while 51.4 percent of girls actively used the tables. Heart rate increased in both genders while using the desks. Interestingly, the girls had a greater increase in heart rate over the boys. Finally, improvements were seen in three out of the four balance tests given. Significant improvement was observed with the left leg and eyes open during the test.

This year our focus was on the effect of balance. Our focus group was a class with quite a few students with ADHD/ADD. Several were on sports teams, but not the majority. Additionally, only one student started out with really good balance. Coincidentally, she was a gymnast and honor roll student.

People take balance for granted but really don't understand the importance of it or how a lack of balance affects the ability to focus. In my class this year, it was evident from the pre-test that the lack of balance would go hand-in-hand with the inability to focus. Prior to beginning the study with the College of Charleston, each student was given a balance test. Dr. Karen Smail hypothesized that there is a strong correlation between good balance and the ability to focus. The students performed the stork balance test and were expected to balance on the ball of their foot with no shoes or socks on a tile floor. Both hands were to remain on their hips while the non-supporting foot remained against the inside knee of the support leg. This pose looks a lot like the "tree" pose in yoga. In general, the results of the balance test were poor, and the average time the students could hold the pose was only three to seven seconds. The positive side to the lack of balance was this would be our area of focus in class.

Students using the kinesthetic tables, as well as the wobble cushions at their seat, showed improved balance over the course of the school year. So what does this mean and what are the implications? I am very excited to say that my students improved their time on task. We will continue this study next year to isolate the variable even more. I know my students looked forward to coming to my class because of the availability of movement.

I have seen such a change in these students throughout the past nine months, and it has been quite a year! Talk about a perfect test group! The students' time on task improved, and they were more engaged with their lessons. There is even more good news—their balance improved too! Was this true in their other classes? Sadly, no but this is actually good news for me.

In classes where students were expected to sit in a traditional desk and still allowed to have a brain blast, it wasn't as significant as using the tables.

Furthermore, the College of Charleston study noted a very telling fact. Even though the students had done brain blasts every thirty minutes, they were still restless and off-task. Asking someone to sit still for thiry minutes can be torture for some kids and adults. It wasn't enough of the right type of movement. Students were allowed to choose to participate and could opt out with a bathroom break or a drink. Thus when they were allowed to take a brain blast, some did not. Therefore, it was difficult for them to reconnect.

CHAPTER THIRTEEN
Dreams Do Come True

I have told you other ways to incorporate movement because I didn't always have the classroom I have now. I started out with a basketball hoop, dancing, yoga, or anything else I could think of to get the students out of their slumber mode.

The idea came to me during the summer of 2012. I thought it would be really cool to have a row of stationary bikes in my classroom, so kids could blow off some steam. School began, and it was time for Open House. At my school, parents expect you to have a bunch of things you want or need for the classroom, written on cute little notes, for you to bring in and donate for the class. Open House night arrived, and I told them I honestly don't want or need anything. Instead, I shared my idea of having bikes. I asked them not to go out and buy one, but if they saw one at a garage sale, I would be glad to pay for it. Or ... if they had one they were using as a laundry hamper, I would take it off their hands. It didn't take long until a mom called me, excited she had found a bike for the class. The kids were THRILLED. It really was the first step of our journey. My next thought was, *how am I going to share one bike with thirty students?* It wasn't actually hard because all of the kids bought into the idea. We decided to use the Smartboard name picker, and students took turns every ten to fifteen minutes on it.

One day my assistant principal, Tiffany Henderson, strolled in the door to conduct an observation. I don't think she was ready to see the bike because it blew her away! She immediately hopped on it and was totally on board with my idea. The next thing I knew, Tiffany brought in another teacher, Lindsay Beck, and she said, "I think there is something you HAVE to see." To say I was excited would be an understatement. Tiffany and I took a road trip the next day to a company nearby, KidsFit. I couldn't believe a place like that existed. It was like my dream of a row of bikes ... on steroids! I informed the owner right then I would purchase it myself, but I had two kids in college, so that wasn't a possibility. At $3,000 per table, it didn't really seem like it was feasible, yet my assistant principal was very excited. Hey, anything was possible!

When I briefed the students about the tables and described how cool they were, they were definitely on board. I showed them one small picture, but they could tell by my excitement this was something amazing! It didn't take very long before I had a donation from a friend of mine, $450 from my Bunco buddy, Kim Uyak, only $2,560 more to go! Then it felt like nothing was happening, and that was the frustrating part. I didn't know HOW to make it happen until one day I received an email.

During that time our school had a new blog, written by our fifth grade students. One of mine had written about the tables, and it had been shown to Dave Spurlock. He was impressed that a ten-year-old was writing about movement. That, my friends, was my light bulb moment. I realized I wasn't actually going to be very successful with this on my own; I was going to need to enlist my fifth graders for help. The next day in class, I threw out an idea to them. "What if we had business lunches to discuss who and how to write to potential donors?" I asked my students. It was strictly voluntary, and a couple of times a week we would meet in my classroom during lunch to learn how to write a business letter and decide to whom we should send it. My students brainstormed tons of names, both locally and nationally (even Warren Buffet. I'm still waiting on that one!)

Parents also came in to proofread. There was definitely a vibe that something big was going on; all of my volunteers were definitely focused. Funny thing is there were a few ADD students in the mix as well, and I think they could sense this being a game changer for their classroom. About the time we were revising, Sloan and her gang (Julia and Brooklyn) decided people were visual, which means a video would probably help. I told them I was already swamped and that they would have to do it themselves. Of course, that didn't matter and probably made it better because it was definitely from a student's perspective. We learned how to create a QR code and put it on the letter itself, very cutting edge for 2013, mind you! Then we waited, but I kept feeling like SOMETHING great was going to happen. About that time Noah, the boy whose mom had found the exercise bike, sold some of his toys on eBay and gave about $65 to the fund. Very sweet and generous for a child to be so giving. Shortly thereafter, we had a few more great moments. A grant I had applied for was given, hooray! Next a donation arrived from two local hospitals (Roper Hospital and Medical University of South Carolina) ... woo hoo!! I could feel the momentum beginning to build; we almost had enough for one table. After speaking to my administration, they recommended giving KidsFit a call to see about a deal for the remainder. In other words, would they work with us? I called the owner of KidsFit, Ed, and I think he saw a bigger picture than I did at the time. Ed told me he really didn't want to see me with one table; he wanted an entire classroom! I hadn't even thought like that! The only stipulation was it was going to cost more. The equipment is very well made; I had never seen anything like it! Back to the drawing board we go. A few more letters, I am guessing probably around twenty-five to thirty were sent during that time and another donation was given, this time by Boeing! It was during this time frame my principal, Leanne Sheppard, saw how committed I was to making this happen. On the day when I was waiting to hear if I made the top five for the district's Teacher of the Year, I found out she would help with the remainder of the costs for the table. This was MUCH better than winning the TOY (Teacher of the Year for the entire district) because this was going to have a major effect on education at my school! I think I literally floated on a cloud afterwards and couldn't wait to tell my babies that it really was going to happen! Finally, the day for the tables to be delivered arrived, and I could barely sleep that night. I felt like a six-year-old child on Christmas Eve; I couldn't wait for morning to come!

From the time I first saw the tables until they were delivered to my classroom, it was only about seven months. I felt incredibly lucky it was that fast. It initially started out as a way to improve my class. I then realized the dream was much bigger than that. What started out being about me then became we. I told my students shortly thereafter that the goal had changed. It was now: school, district, state, and nation. My amazing students moved on without me to sixth grade, and now I was tasked with having a new set of students. Would they appreciate what the former students had done? Would they take care of these amazing tables? How would I keep the momentum going to have the new students care as much as the previous class had? I decided I would have to teach them WHY it was important and what their role would be in this journey.

As we were getting to know one another at the beginning of the new school year, people were starting to tour our classroom, and the word was starting to spread! Soon Coke, yes that company, wanted to come and check it out. I was on cloud nine! They seemed very interested but wanted a video. Sound familiar? I informed my class and of course, they were on board! Being a teacher, I gave them a few guidelines but left it to them to create and create they did, during recess several times a week and then they polished and tweaked it. Their final product was pretty amazing and even more amazing is how many views we received on School Tube, over 9,500 views! I have since moved it to YouTube, as I had some problems with the School Tube not working and needed it to be reliable for presentations. We waited and then waited some more; it was almost like we would have something exciting happen and then nothing. Change doesn't happen overnight! Why am I telling you this? I know you are anxious for things to happen in your classroom, I totally get that and I was there myself. I now feel the same way about the rest of my goal. I want it to happen everywhere. I find it discouraging we use traditional desks when we have such a gold mine within our reach! My analogy is this: we spend money all the time on curriculum and technology that is ever-changing. It always requires more money; these tables give so much more and do not require an update. We have tried everything else to improve education, why not let students move and help them learn in a more productive way?

I will now step off the soapbox, sorry, kinda, not really ... what can I say? It's my passion, and I believe in it with my whole heart!

CHAPTER FOURTEEN

Classroom Management With Your New Room

Students Unfamiliar with the Tables

Meet the Teacher is another time when people who aren't familiar with the equipment are in the classroom. I always ask people to be safe when younger siblings come in and to keep an eye on them. The tables are well made and heavy, but still need to be treated with respect. If a young child does not know how to use the tables correctly, he or she could get hurt. It would be their fault, but we don't want that to happen.

One thing I will do differently this year is to create mini-posters of a student utilizing the desk for each table or station. It will be a quick way for the new students (and their siblings) to get acquainted with them and see how they should use them properly. Of course, I will laminate them to use the first few weeks of school or when we have a new student.

Their Point of View

If I were to guess, this is the chapter most teachers would go to first. Many might think, how in the world do you manage this type of classroom? How do you get the students to behave? Just like anything else: practice, practice, practice OR procedure, procedure, procedure. I will admit that I was a little apprehensive at first because it was just so new, so different! The students and I sat down the very first day and discussed the novelty of it. I asked them to imagine what it would be like if their parents suddenly gave them a jump castle for a bed! The students' eyes lit up. This type of classroom is an adventure. Put yourself in their shoes.

I wanted to talk to the students about how to best take care of our new classroom, to ensure learning was still going to happen. The students and I discussed what their vision was for the classroom using sticky notes. They worked in groups to decide what the room should sound and look like. Mind you, this was from their perspective and important in creating an environment conducive to learning, as well as helping them "own their classroom". Afterwards, we created a poster of their rules or "Standard Operating Procedures" and all of the students signed it. Mind you, if there are issues later on and you realize something isn't working, that is a perfect opportunity to convene for a quick meeting and see what needs to be changed or fine-tuned.

This is a wonderful way to have them hold each other accountable for the rules they have created, and then it doesn't have to be your responsibility to be "Classroom Cop".

What if They Don't Feel Well and Don't Want to Stand?
Many teachers ask what I do for students who don't want to stand. I have not seen it as a problem during the two years I

have had the tables, but I have always told the students it is okay to switch with a person at a seated station. I also have several traditional science tables and wobble cushions for the rug that they can sit on as well. There are definitely options available, and you should ensure you have options too, just in case. I am very flexible when it comes to a student who doesn't feel well. However, there are many students who are used to sitting all the time. For these children, constant movement might take a little getting used to—unfortunately, we live in sedentary world. Sitting is the new smoking. This too shall pass.

Noises and Responsibility

As any elementary student will tell you, simple machines will encounter friction. They probably won't say it like that, but they understand the concept of something rubbing against something else. The tables really aren't loud, but once in a while, we will hear a squeak. I used this opportunity to talk about friction and opposing forces. Hey, it was a teachable moment, I couldn't resist! Then I put some lubricant on it, and all was good in the world again. When this happened a few months later, one of my "Mr. or Miss Fix It" students in the classroom took care of it for me. Life is good, and I love when my kids are actively taking care of the classroom and me. However if it is more than a squeak, I would contact the company you purchased it from so they can help you with the issue.

Besides having a student in charge of noises, I also have one vacuum the foot pedals on the elliptical. I bought a mini-vacuum, which does a fantastic job of cleaning hard-to-reach areas, so our after-school cleaning crew doesn't have to deal with the mess.

Listening to Instructions

If I really want to make sure my students hear what I say, I ask the ones that are on the standing stations to step off. Asking for their eyes on me also helps. Another strategy is to call the students onto the carpet and discuss expectations. Honestly, this isn't what I normally have to do, but it is helpful when the students are first becoming acclimated to the tables.

Out of the Room

What do you do? Unless you have the moonwalker, it really isn't an issue. I consider the tables to be well made, but you do need to use them respectfully, especially the moonwalker, you can really get some air on it! I ask the students to step off when I leave the room and to stand by the table instead. Since I am always trying out new equipment for you teachers, I don't have one now, and it really isn't an issue. If you are concerned with liability issues, then simply have the students step off the tables.

Things That Will Drive You Crazy

I know I should be positive but hey, let's be real. When I first saw them on the desks, it was actually hilarious; they looked like hamsters on a hamster wheel. I asked them if it bothered them, of course they said, "no" as they happily moved and bobbed up and down. I think watching the movement was harder for me than it was for them. No truer words spoken but get over yourself, this is about them moving! Over time it became easier for me to look at them. Oh, one more thing ... I am not sure why they do it, but it might drive you crazy at first. They always look at their feet. After a while, I applied the humor technique and would ask them if their feet were still there. They look at me as if I am crazy and reply, "Yes." I always say, "Thank goodness!" They get the joke and then try to not look at their feet for a while. It takes some time, as it is a novelty, but it does pass.

Since I have attention issues (and control issues), it is important for me to know they know what to do when I give instructions. Sometimes I ask the students to step off the tables and look directly at me while I speak. I sometimes also ask them to come to the rug but not as much anymore. Like I said, that is more my problem than theirs.

I asked my colleagues what went on in their room and Amy Ryan, fourth grade teacher, stated: "What I did notice last year was that sometimes it appeared that students weren't interested in the bikes unless friends were on the bikes with them. I am trying to figure out a system to combat that problem for this year. A few students were actually more distracted on the bikes. They would constantly disrupt class by getting up to get materials throughout the day or may use the bikes inappropriately by standing up or sitting sideways." This is more of a problem when you have a limited amount of kinesthetic desks.

Standardized Testing

How I handle standardized testing is a question I am asked the most, besides seating arrangements. In our testing manual it states, "Students seating environment should be the same as what they are used to having in their classroom." That is not a problem; it is exactly how I have mine! I realize every state has different procedures for the test-taking environment. My suggestion is to plan early and be proactive. I purchased privacy shields from Really Good Stuff, and it was well worth the investment. It is important to have the support of your administration too. Brainstorm with them early on to make sure you are both on the same page. It hasn't been a problem for me, but I have heard it might be a concern for some. As time goes on and these tables become the norm, I don't see it being a problem for testing.

Acting a Fool!

Just as you see kids tip back in their conventional chairs, sometimes this applies to the tables as well. My students KNOW the rules because we created them the first day. However, kids will be kids. If I see a child using a station/ seat inappropriately, I do what any other teacher would do, I use proximity. If it appears to be a problem, I remind them of the rules they created for their safety and redirect them to another station. The students know that I mean business, and we are here to learn, have fun, and move ... darn it, and NOT act a fool!

Seating Chart

I try to be fair with the kinesthetic tables. I have all different kinds of stations so, of course, everyone has their favorite, and they want to get to that one first. My first strategy was to use the sit down tables one week, and then utilize the standing stations one week. It worked, kind of, but then I realized some kids weren't being fair and going to certain ones they liked. That has definitely been a work in progress, and I thought I had finally found what works for me. Actually, I was running out of ideas, and the kids came up with it; students really do have a lot of great ideas! Second strategy: students will start off at a certain table (with their established seating chart) and then move to the next table the following week. Whatever seat they are using, they use that seat for the remainder of the week. I like this because it ensures each child will get the opportunity to try each seat out and not have to wait forever for a particular table. Mondays take them a few minutes to figure it out, but it works and of course, you always have a few sheepdogs to lead the rest. Mind you, whoever was sitting next to them that week will still be to the right and left of them in the same order every time. That system helps them remember where to sit. Although I am okay with our seating arrangement, and I enjoy watching the kids figure it out for themselves. That is part of the process for kids to work with others. Third theory: As I type this, I thought, you could always have the students at a certain table for a month, and so that is what we tried next. As much as I wanted them to "try out" different stations, it was too much to remember when we needed to get down to the business of learning. For me, having the students at the same seat for a quarter (or a month) is much more manageable. I mean, seriously, who has time to constantly make new seating arrangements?

Ultimately, you have to do what works best for you. I am only telling you what I have done so you can suffer less; really I give to the end, people. If you have a system you like better, go for it and then tell me. You can also alleviate the hassle and have all of the same type of kinesthetic stations/tables, and then this won't be an issue.

Perspectives From Another Teacher

Amy Ryan gave me some additional feedback on how she handles things in her classroom. She said, "I have two bicycle tables in my room. This allows four students to be on the bikes at a time. My classroom is self-contained, so I rotate through four new students each day. I post the schedule every Monday. If it is their day, students have the option of being on the bike the whole day. Some students clear out their desk and bring all of their things to the bike table for the day. While others go to the table at certain points during the day. I leave it up to them. Some students choose to pass on the bikes altogether. If a student is absent, I just move them to the next day and put another child on the bike. Overall, students are very excited about the bikes. My observation during the day is that students bike more when doing independent work. When listening to instruction, they often seem to stop biking. When they are on the bikes all day, they are not biking all day just off and on."

CHAPTER FIFTEEN

It's a Tool Too?

Wan do you mean it's a tool? It's a desk, for goodness sake!
Well, yes and no. It is a tool for several reasons.

"Use the Force, Luke."

First, these kinesthetic tables are a tool to help "channel" the energy our students have. I have some students I allow to come in early with the expectation they can pedal their little hearts out. They are NOT talking to me because I am preparing for my school day. They are NOT doing schoolwork because that is what they do all day long. It is enticing to these kids to know there are no expectations, except to move. I know it sounds crazy, but I guess the best way to compare it is if you are working out and you can "zone out" during the moment. They are focused solely on moving, and it helps get the urge to move out of their system.

Crickets

Ever looked at your students while you are teaching and swear you hear crickets? Most of us have, and it is because we have lost their attention. Kids, and adults, can only pay attention for so long before they disconnect. A great way to use the tables (if you have them) is to play some music at 180 BPM (beats per minute). Do this for one or two minutes at most. You don't have to have kinesthetic tables in order to do this, just have the students stand up and move!

With the tables, I sometimes will have them move as fast as they safely can do so, of course holding on as they go. I like to play something like, "Eye of the Tiger" or some other fast song.

As an alternative to moving on the tables, which they love, step off and dance! My students love the Macarena, the Chicken Dance (I sing it REALLY fast), and the Sid Shuffle (I like to Move It, Move It). With or without the tables, you don't have to complete an entire song; one minute is enough time to raise the heart rate. Look at it this way, taking the time to stop for one or two minutes, gives you MORE time to teach. The students have had the opportunity to get their sillies out and are ready for learning. It was a purposeful movement blast and a side benefit? Everyone is smiling.

Movement Creates Pathways in the Brain

Although I love to have the kids use the tables, as well as dance and walk laps, movement really should be more purposeful. I recently heard the question posed, "Can you learn algebra by listening to directions?" Conversely, you could ask someone, "How did you learn to change a light bulb?" The answer to that question instantly pops in our head; we learned how to change a light bulb by doing it! The theory applies to learning concepts more deeply than merely memorizing the facts for a brief time. As I sat in Paul Zientarski and Scott Miller's class, I saw firsthand how they used movement to make abstract ideas, in math, become more concrete. For example, we first briefly discussed angles in geometry and then created these same angles with pipe cleaners. We were encouraged to confer with one another on whether we had indeed created the angle, as well as justify why it was the particular angle. More movement followed as we then used our bodies to create the angles we had previously reviewed before moving on to more complex angles: complimentary and supplementary. The more we used the movement to create the angles and discuss the properties of the angles, the greater our ability to retain the information. The same thing happens when you see someone change a light bulb or complete any other physical task. You learn it by doing the task. Why should learning subjects in school be any different?

Another thing I noticed while completing the "pipe cleaner" and "arm geometry" activities, it made my peers and me smile. I love that! I want my students to be happy and engaged, while moving. Cassie Connor is another amazing teacher, who is a pioneer of movement in the classroom. She can take any ordinary object and make it fun! One example she showed me was her "alligator binder". Although she uses it for her four-year-old class, I could easily see adapting and changing it for my fifth grade students. She has a binder with an alligator on the cover and inside it has all 3D objects. Cassie also has other concepts and very easily changes out 3D for colors, numbers, or whatever she is currently teaching in her class. Her game is simple but fun: she opens up the binder quickly and you have to identify the shape before the "alligator" snaps the binder shut. I can see little ones laughing hysterically at that; it really speaks to them! When I first saw it, I dismissed it as being too immature for my "big" fifth grade students. Really? What was I thinking? This fun idea can be used easily from Pre-K through fifth grade, and you can bet I WILL be using this idea. I see this as a center idea; where students could work together and take turns as the alligator. If you did this with a student, you could easily see if they under-stand the concept and not even have to grade a paper. Simply by playing an easy game in less than five minutes, you can learn which students need remediation. I love this because it prevents students from slipping further behind. As if you needed another reason why this is awesome, think about the movement that occurs during the activity. Student's thinking is reinforced, and they are able to picture the answer to the question. I walked away from Cassie VERY impressed!

Class Participation

Want to know if your kids understand a concept? Use your tables to help them show you. During the course of teaching Sir Isaac Newton's Three Laws of Motion, I told them they could use anything in the classroom to demonstrate it on a video. Several of my students used the pedals from the elliptical station to demonstrate understanding. I loved it, because I could assess immediately they had mastered the material.

Although Newton's Laws of Motion may not be part of your curriculum, there could be some way to use the tables to show understanding. For example, when working with fractions, I asked my students to pedal forward if the answer was in simplest form. If the fraction needed to be reduced, they had to pedal backward. Everyone is moving, so unless a student is not pedaling and looking to see what his or her peers are doing, I can tell who understands and who doesn't. Also, if they are looking around, that gives me a big indication I need to give some one-on-one time. For those pedaling the wrong way, I now know I need to teach again, as that is just as important for them to learn it correctly.

Using the stations as a tool is something I constantly strive to include more in my teaching day. For younger grades, it could be even or odd numbers and moving. Perhaps move if it is even and pause if it is odd. During Language Arts, students could have a beat, or cadence, as they say their spelling words. For older students, moving in a certain direction if a number is prime or composite, if something is biotic or abiotic, and the list goes on!

Saving Face

One of the classes I teach consists of the top five percent of the entire grade level. These kids would never admit they don't understand a math concept. They are used to always knowing the answer and being the smartest kids in the class. I love it because I can tell when they are struggling. Wait, that doesn't sound right, it makes it sound like I am sadistic. What I mean to say is, I love it when there is a way for me to understand they are struggling and help them save face at the same time. Most of the time, my kids are constantly moving, even if it is a slight movement. The neat thing that my friend, Dave Spurlock, pointed out to me was when they don't move and what that means. Students will pause when they are really focused and trying to figure out the problem. As I said before, these same kids would never before tell me if they didn't understand something. Now I can easily scan the room and go up to the individual to ask if they need help. It is surprising when I ask them if they need help, they look relieved and amazed I know they need help. Just like that, more learning has occurred. I love those moments!

CHAPTER SIXTEEN
Purposeful Movement

After I had my dream classroom set up, I opened it up for any and all to see. I was thrilled and wanted to share my vision of what a class could and should look like! Many a time parents would marvel and say things like, "I wish they would have had something like this when I was growing up!" Or another statement I heard a lot was, "My son (or daughter) would really benefit from this type of movement." That made me feel validated and happy to know parents were supportive and behind this movement. It was about this time my glass half-empty husband gave me something to think about. He said, "Be careful, or your whole class will be full of ADHD kids." He didn't mean that in a mean way, but he did have a valid point. As they said in the movie, Field of Dreams, "If you build it, they will come." I started thinking about what he said and was honestly a little nervous. I know it sounds hypocritical, but I didn't want a class full of ADHD students. I am fine with some but having too many would be pandemonium! So just to make sure before the beginning of the school year, I reminded my administration we needed to be mindful of numbers with regard to numbers in my classroom, meaning spread the proportion of students with ADHD. I did that for two years in a row because I was afraid of chaos. This past August, I forgot to make that request known to the front office. I figured it didn't matter at this point, they knew and I knew I had requested it before. Why should I need to say anything more? I was excited about the upcoming school year with my teaching partner, Laura Murphy. The previous year had been our first together and her first year of teaching. The girl is a dynamo, willing to jump into the concept of kinesthetic learning, brain blasts, or anything else I threw her way! We came together to plan for the school year, excited about all we would conquer together. It was a beautiful plan, and our theme was going to be #bestyearever. I think that was the moment when we jinxed our school year and ourselves.

Our first day of school finally arrives! I am excited to meet our students and begin the year learning together. It is 5am, and it feels like it is 4pm on a Friday at a local happy hour. I am looking around thinking, *I am reliving what all teachers dream about during the summer.* Students are usually quiet when they come in, you know, the whole "I don't know what to expect" mindset. Little did I know then, many of them already knew each other and more than a few were diagnosed with ADHD/ADD, as well as those who were not diagnosed with the disorder but seemed very bouncy. Now after I tell you this, I know what you are thinking, "Why would I want to have this happen in my classroom?" As much as I would like to keep my affairs private, this really needs to be shared. We learn just as much (or more) from what goes wrong as we do from what goes right. I think I had all those students for a reason, and it was probably to tell others how to learn from it.

In every classroom there will be students with ADHD/ADD, as more and more students are diagnosed with it. Administrators need to be mindful of this when assigning classroom rosters for the upcoming school year. I say this because as helpful and useful as the kinesthetic tables are, there is a problem with too many kids with attention issues in one classroom. They actually distract each other from paying attention, including their ADD teacher! It is almost as if there is too much stimuli with all of ADHD kids and the tables. Is it a problem with five kids? No. When there are ten or more, it is more of an issue. I am not saying this to scare anyone off, but it is something we need to be mindful of when assigning class lists. It is also another reason why it would be very helpful to have them in every classroom. If that isn't a reality at this point, then having a table in several teachers' rooms would be an option for equally distributing the numbers of students with attention issues. Please know this, I am not saying it doesn't work with a lot of ADHD students, but it is important to know they can be over stimulated by each other.

What happens if it happens to you? There were many things I tried to help reign in my sweet kids. Obviously, the first thing is to not have them sitting next to each other but then again, that is a given. The only problem is when they are at every table, and you don't have that option. Besides seating charts, I used the standard behavior charts that all teachers do. Unfortunately, it didn't really help as much as I had hoped it would. My partner and I gave out a more in-depth interest survey so we could see what motivates them. We used the information as incentives and began using Class Dojo. That did seem to help some, but it wasn't the answer.

I noticed their attention span was about ten minutes, maybe fifteen minutes if I stretched it. The class period was just too long, even with kinesthetic tables. Then I had my first of many brainstorms! We would set the timer for fifteen minutes and do a quick brain blast to help re-engage them. This went against everything I wanted to do. Why should I when the students have these fabulous tables to use already? ADHD students love new things but they can grow bored of it after a while; they like things switched up a bit and appreciate variety, as we all do. I can definitely attest to this, as I have seen it a lot this year.

It seems like what worked for a little while doesn't always hold their interest. So as fabulous as the tables worked, I knew these kids needed for me to shake it up a bit and incorporate some purposeful movement. The first activity I did was just to put on some music and have them go as fast as they could while a fast song was playing. Imagine a spin class and I was doing it at the same time, cheering them on for one minute. It made the whole class smile. My advice is to look for music with clean lyrics and a fast tempo, preferably about 180 BPM.

After a while, I started using whole brain teaching. Research shows students learn best by doing; we knew that already. I started teaching in smaller segments. I would teach one concept to the class, then have them turn and teach it to each other. This gave me instant feedback on how much they understood. I also had the opportunity to observe them teach each other. The best part? They were given the opportunity to talk and NOT get in trouble. Another thing I liked about it, the same students weren't the ones with their hands raised. Everyone had the chance to have their ideas heard. An added benefit was the students seemed to like it too, and it especially helped my ADHD students.

As much as I like using active teaching, I wanted to change it up even more. I had never felt like I was very successful at incorporating centers and wanted to do this with my kids. Besides researching on the Internet, I visited several classrooms and observed how to successfully incorporate it into mine. I decided to have three centers and have the students move every fifteen minutes. The students used the tables for a particular center. They were able to sit/stand at stations they normally did not sit at and were allowed to move to another after fifteen minutes. Their learning continued, and the students were more on task

84

than I had ever seen them. I was starting to feel as though I may be on to something! From the feedback the students gave me, they liked learning with one another in pairs/small groups. They also appreciate knowing they will be moving in a short amount of time. It also helps them to use their time more efficiently, so they can finish the task at hand. They know otherwise it would be unfinished work and something they would have to take home for homework. ADHD students like knowing there is a time limit; it helps those who tend to procrastinate to get going, as there is a sense of urgency.

Now the centers seem to be going well, I am getting to know my students and yes, they have calmed down tremendously from the beginning of the year. However, it is still no walk in the park. I have to tweak it a bit more because now spring is in the air and these kids remind me of Thing One and Thing Two from the book, *The Cat in the Hat*. I thought to myself, what am I going to do with them? Then I realized my elliptical stations have a tension dial on them! As soon as some of my students come in the next morning, I tell them I am doing an experiment that involves having them move for the next five minutes without doing any work. They look at me like I am crazy, but who is going to argue with a teacher telling them not to work? After a while, they are actually getting winded and tired. Imagine that. I switch them out and let other students get on them. Soon, they all want their turn, including those who don't have noticeable attention issues. After they complete their five minutes, the students have calmed down and are now ready to work. Prior to this, they would occasionally pedal a bit, or perhaps stand at the top of it and just perch, like a bird. (I kid you not.) Now by using the elliptical as it was meant to be used, and exerting their energy, they were in a proper frame of mind to focus. This, my friends, is what I mean by purposeful movement. The five minutes I asked of them was worth it if you knew these sparkling individuals.

Because I do not have tension on every station and my students like it when I change up our routine, the beginning of spring was the perfect opportunity to get them outside and clear their mind. There is a bus loop right outside our classroom, and spring had definitely sprung. My kids were EXTRA excited! It felt as though I needed to do something different, so outside we went. Don't get me wrong, I am thrilled and honored to have the most amazing classroom. I do think it is important to monitor and adjust though. We are only held back by our choices, and there are tons! I laced up my shoes as well, and we set up our "track". The goal was to run on the first half and if need be, walk or skip on the right side. This is a great way to help the students develop into runners without feeling they couldn't do it if they didn't run the entire lap. Another added benefit is for the students who may have had issues at home in the morning or an incident on the bus. How can you be mad and skip? I don't think it is possible. As a motivational tool, I periodically ask the students to write on Edmodo (a social educational website) how many laps they completed. I tell the students to not worry about what other students do, they are competing against themselves. Then I give them the same amount of Dojo points. I created a positive behavior point for this and award the number of laps they complete. Thus, three laps equals three positive Dojo points, to be redeemed at a later time. That really gets them excited, but it is sporadic, so they never know when it is going to happen. An interesting observation I am starting to see is how my "non-runners" are starting to run. It is also an opportunity to model by example, as well as talk with my students. One in particular, Martin, surprised me by how well he ran. It was a great opportunity for us to connect in a way we had not done before, as he is somewhat reserved. I was also surprised by the students who are so hyper but not so much while we run. This is a time they should be using up all the energy they save for the classroom. A little quiet encouragement lets them know I am running along with them, and the movement we are doing will help them in the classroom.

Here is my little nugget that I really want you to get and forgive me if you already do, the students who have all of this energy aren't moving and they should be. If they were, there would not be as much disruption in the classroom. From the observations I have seen thus far, it isn't usually the students who are outside all the time playing or who play in sports. It is the ones who do not move enough. You know it is true when you have had a great workout; you are ready to calm down and just relax. However, what happens if you don't play on a team or don't get your excitement out? What if you sit a lot at home? The energy is going to come out somewhere; I would lay odds on that because there is no game system at school or television. Then suddenly, the "active" switch is on! What does this mean? We have to help the students release that energy, in order to help them prepare their minds and bodies for learning. If we don't help students release their energy, it will become evident sooner than later.

So why is it that I told you all of the things I tried in the classroom? I did this to let you know several things. First, you are not alone. You are a trailblazer! Sounds pretty impressive, huh? Until having kinesthetic tables are the "norm" for classrooms, students will be excited about it and yes, there may be a year when you have a few more ADHD kids than you normally have had. Second, I want you to think outside of the box and find something that works for you and your students. I wanted my students engaged and excited about learning. I will do whatever it takes to help them, as I know you would too. Third, this part is for administration; it is imperative classes are divided up equally and fairly. As much as these tables really do help all students, it is somewhat diminished and unfair when they are too many in one class. Please be mindful of that when planning. The good news for me is we now have tables in three other classes for next fall. Woo hoo! That means when a parent requests me because the tables would "help" her son or daughter, the students will be divided up among all classes with the tables. The truth is, the tables help all students. We just need to make sure we have them in every classroom.

Disclaimer: This reference to the classroom was only for the sake of teaching others. This teacher accepts no liability for assumptions made by former parents. The students with ADHD were anonymous and never labeled by name orally or in written form. Please note that any views or opinions presented in this book are solely those of the author and do not necessarily represent those of the school district.

CHAPTER SEVENTEEN
Administrators, This Is for You Too!

This may look slightly familiar to you because you just read something very similar. However, I am doing this to make a point. Movement needs to occur in EVERY classroom. So for the sake of sounding redundant, I will say it in another format:

As wonderful as the kinesthetic tables are, there is a drawback that you really need to be mindful of and this where I need administrators to really hear me. Everything was fine the first couple of years but of course ... good news spreads, and that is what I wanted to happen. However, I had this nagging feeling in the back of my mind and all the while my husband kept saying, "They (administrators) are going to give you all the hyper students." I told him repeatedly that it wouldn't happen and of course, just to cover myself, I reminded my principal to be mindful of that each summer, until this past summer. I forgot to remind her. I remember getting pumped up for my upcoming school year and thinking it would be the #bestyearever! The first few minutes of the first day told me that it was going to be a challenge.

I know what you are thinking and yes, I did want the tables and I am not sorry. I think I am not the norm with this scenario. I am not the norm period. I wave my freak flag quite high and proud, thank you very much! Most people do not have an entire class set. I tell the students we are like a showroom for people to come see what a full kinesthetic classroom could look like. At the beginning of the year, there was only one other teacher who had a table. When a concept is new, it requires an adjustment period. Then when more teachers have the tables in their rooms, administrators will be able to "spread the love" or in other words parcel out the students more equitably. Part of this is just the nature of being a teacher; former parents request me for their upcoming siblings and that is a beautiful thing.

All I am asking from administrators is to be mindful of the distribution of students. We need kinesthetic desks in every classroom, and then this really won't be an issue. Oh and just for sake of closure, even with a "high octane" class this year, it truly was the #bestyearever. It is how we choose to look at things and our attitude. I believe I was given these students for a reason and part of that would be to help you as well. The next chapter deals with how to make the most of what you have been given. Maybe I should have called it "When Life Gives You Lemons".

CHAPTER EIGHTEEN
The Next Step in Adding More Movement

When about a one third of the class has attention issues, I needed to come up with a new plan and fast! One of the things I did was to invite students to come in early just to use the elliptical. I wanted them to not do any work but focus on going as fast and hard as they could for five minutes. They were sweating and out of breath, it was beautiful! It did help calm them down, and that was a motivating factor for me. You don't have to ask them to come into class early, but perhaps as soon as students arrive in the morning, put the really "active" students on the desks where they are using their larger muscles. Another use for the elliptical was to switch out my students, as I only had four of that particular station. Students looked forward to being on them, and it helped divert their attention, recharge, and refocus. It really was hilarious to watch them going 100 mph.

I knew movement was important but my epiphany was realizing students also needed to raise their heart rate. Just moving was fine but not as effective. When I had the students increase their level of movement, I noticed a change in their behavior. They seemed calmer than before, able to focus, and my boys were smiling more! I then remembered what Dave Spurlock had said about the 180 BPM. Why had I forgotten that important piece of the puzzle? No matter, you remember when you are supposed to, and I guess that was my moment. Instantly, I added music to the mix when we needed a brain blast. I would crank up the tunes for one or two minutes. Sometimes I only had time for a minute and would tell the students to move as fast as they could during that time. Then other times we would switch seats after thirty seconds, so they could use another station. The effects were instantaneous. And no, the students weren't crazy after that. Remember the "egg of calmness"? I would instantly use that afterwards, and we would go back to whatever we were doing.

The egg of calmness isn't something to do at the beginning of the school year, it is a procedure I use the entire school year. It works, and they calm down very quickly. You have to tell them they will have a short brain blast and walk them through the steps. This will let the students know the expectations, as well as what will occur. For example, I would tell my students something like this, "Class, you need a brain blast. We are going to hold onto the tables and move as fast as we can for sixty seconds. When you hear the music pause, switch to the seat to your left. When you hear the music stop, you stop and look at me. We will do the egg of calmness and return to our work." Say whatever you want to say, but keep it brief. I would continue practicing that until they know it very well. I have done brain blasts with visitors in the room, and it isn't a big deal. The students act accordingly because they have practiced the procedure.

Now I was getting excited with these kids because I am actually seeing a difference and they seem to be able to focus more with the increased movement. The next thing I remembered was the book, Spark, and how students would come to school and work out before they started their school day. One morning I came in, and told the kids to line up to go outside. They asked me if they had done anything wrong. What? Why do kids always think they have done something wrong? I told them no, I just realized we needed to start our day off on a better note. The only instructions I gave them were to run, and if they couldn't do that the whole time, skipping or power walking was fine. It is important to remember though to lead by example. If you only say they should do this and you don't, then I think it looks hypocritical to the students. That is my opinion though, so you be you. However, I do know kids are very observant, and it means a lot to see the teacher is out there running laps with them. Did I do it in a dress? You bet! I wore biking shorts underneath and would change into my running shoes. Does that mean you have to run in a dress or a tie? No, and I didn't run every day ... sometimes I skipped. The running/skipping/power walking became our morning routine every day and even before state testing. After a run, we would go inside to begin class. The instructions were to send me a short post on Edmodo.com to let me know how many laps they completed. It was a way of having accountability for them and for me. I also used Edmodo to model healthy physical activity, as well as get a peek into my student's lives. For example, on Sunday evening I sometimes would write them a note and ask them what physical activities they engaged in during the weekend. It wasn't about gloating by telling them all I had done. I would also take the time to be real with them and let them know I wanted to be a sloth but knew I needed to get my butt out there and run through the puddles. I liked sharing with them because then I already had a glimpse of their weekend, and it was great for building community as well.

CHAPTER NINETEEN
Can We Kick This Up a Notch?

Momentum is building, things are getting better but I still felt like I wanted to use the tables in a more purposeful way. Ed Pinney, KidsFit, and I got together and brainstormed what we could do to create a brain blast using the stations. Obviously, tweak as you wish, these are only suggestions.

On Station Warm Up
This is done on whatever station you are currently using:

1. Move back and forth to the count of ten, or whatever it does, by that I mean use the station the way you normally would. Every stretch listed here we did for a count of ten. Alter this to work for you.
2. Touch alternating knees.

3. In this stretch, the student twists to the left and holds it for a count of ten. Then, they repeat the stretch to the right.

4. Hands overhead and stretch back for a count of ten. I tell my students to pretend they are puppets; to imagine strings at the tips of their fingers suspending them.

5. Over shoulder neck stretch. With the over shoulder neck stretch, your body remains static and only your head moves. You should be looking over your right shoulder and then repeat with your left shoulder.

6. Touch shoulder blades. During this stretch, pull your arms back as she has done, then try to touch your elbows together and feel the resistance.

Next, Step Off the Equipment
Keep one hand on the table and one hand on your hip. Feet shoulder width apart. Then count to ten while doing deep knee bends (squats), three seconds down and three seconds coming up. Make sure to pause in down position for an added stretch.

Now It Is Really Time To Turn It Up!

Here are individual stretches for each station. I will tell you when we started these, we did three of each. After a while though, my fifth graders suggested we increase the time to six seconds for each part. Do what works for you and your students.

Alternating Lunges

Do ten of these between each station. Have the students count it off and give you a break. Sharing the job of keeping track helps them to buy into the movement as well.

Strider

At this station, you want to accentuate the movement. Have the student contract their muscles and hold for a count of three then switch legs. The best way to describe it is you are suspended in one direction. Once students get used to doing this, you can have them answer math facts.

Balance Board

Start with the heel down, then lift up and tighten the calf for six seconds. Continue this motion of up for three and down for three for ten counts. This may seem easy which is why it is important to contract the calf muscles and really use them to feel the effect. First, stand on backs of heels. Then, reverse and push weight forward.

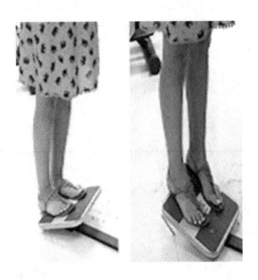

Elliptical

I call this one the "speed skater" because the form looks somewhat similar to that. While moving the feet, look in one direction with your head down. Feel the tightening in the abdominal muscles as you twist to one side. Then repeat on the other side for a count of ten.

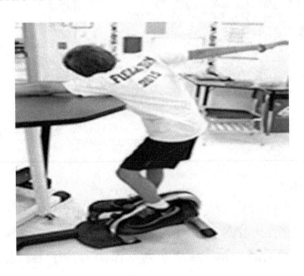

Hula

I call this station the hula because you have a slight side-to-side movement. However for this particular stretch, I have the students do what is called "crane". Remember the scene from Karate Kid? The student tightens the leg they are standing on to make it solid. Then they keep their balance while keeping the other leg up and elevated with a bent knee. After holding this pose for three seconds, then switch to the other side. You can face away from the table or towards the table. I also remind them to tighten their core as they do this.

Bicycle

For this station, the student uses resistance bands. They push up, similar to a military press, to the count of three. Then, very slowly, they release the resistance bands to the count of three while they are pedaling.

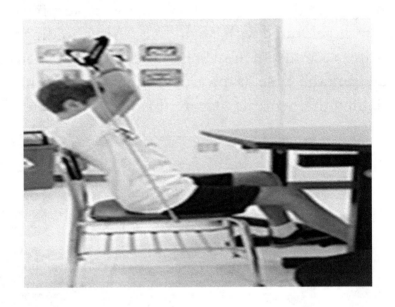

Kneeling Spinner

The student must be in a plank position and facing forward. They twist to the left for three seconds and then alternate to the right for three seconds. It is important to have a tight core, especially their bottom while completing this exercise. Look at this fabulous plank form even while in his graduation suit!

Pogo Seat

This is a great exercise for the triceps. As teachers get older they should be required to do this one to keep the "bat wings" at bay. You know what those are, the floppy skin under the arm. I shiver thinking about it! For correct position, the student should kneel with the seat between their legs. Then they push down on the seat for a slow count of three. Afterwards the seat is released, and the student slowly counts to three to bring the seat to the original position. Important, remember to keep the abs contracted while doing this exercise. This is a little hard to visualize, so here are both steps. First, straddle hands and press down slowly. Then, release slowly into the up position.

 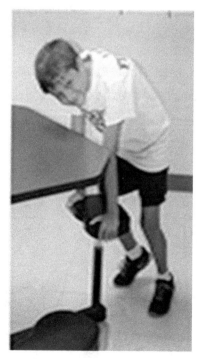

In my opinion, it is important to let the students have a voice in these stretches. Together, we decide what we like or what needs to be changed. My students came up with a few more to use too.

Finn starts in the middle in the squat position. He moves to the left and holds that for a count of three, then repeats on the right. Of course, this is done for ten times too. I especially like this one because it helps students work on their balance.

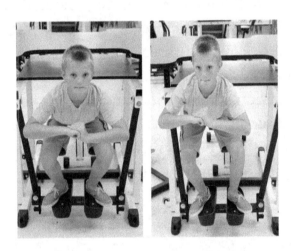

Mia starts in the standing, pushup position. Slowly, she moves as we count to three, Mia pushes towards the table as she feels the resistance. She then returns to the starting position as she counts to three.

What Does This Look Like?

Are we doing this for an extended amount of time? No, you are adding resistance to your quick brain blast and using the equipment to your advantage. You have to use what works for you. How I usually did mine was a little different than what you may imagine. For me, we start out with the on station warm up I told you about first. Then the students step off and go to the first station, not the one they originally sat at and are assigned to use on a regular basis. They would perform the stretch with the entire class together. I usually count for them to lead the pace. It is also a teachable moment because I am doing it with them, not just telling them to do it. Students buy into it a lot more when they feel you are in it with them. Once they have finished their stretch on that particular station, they step off and we do lunges together. Personally, I HATE lunges, so this is a great way for me to get my workout in too! With the lunges, I let a student count that one out, and they seem to like doing that. I call out the station ones, just because I have a certain pace I want them to follow. Once we have belted out ten lunges, we move to the next station and perform it together. This is then followed by ten more lunges. I don't go through the entire series because I do have to teach. However, you could do two or three until everyone is energized. Then, later on, say in about fifteen to thirty minutes, do another one so the students can complete ones they hadn't done before. I will tell you I don't like pandemonium or things that will stop me from completing my task of teaching. We really don't have enough time in the day. However, if you create a classroom climate and students feel safe enough to say, "I need a brain blast", it will pay off BIG TIME! What I described to you I do very quickly, and it is usually about three minutes, which is the same as a GoNoodle dance video. Granted, I love a good dance video but not every one does. Also, I feel resistance is an essential part to getting the "wiggles" out. Lame word but you know what I mean.

My advice to you is to model as you would anything else. Practice and at first, only do the warm up. Do this in baby steps, I definitely took it slow. Next, add on the stretch for one particular station.

Of course, you will have to model it for each station so everyone knows what to do. I would next do the basic stretch and one station. Next add on a lunge, the students seem to love the lunges. They are the transition to the next station. Like I mentioned earlier, have a student call out the lunge count. They love doing that, as it gives them a role in this activity. When you feel they are ready, add another station afterwards. Honestly, I usually only did two or three stations for each brain blast returning back to work. Sometimes you just need a little pause to re-energize. For example, when I stop what I am doing to go to the teacher workroom to use the copy machine or bathroom, I come back with amazing ideas. I often wondered why that was. Now I know, because I allowed myself a moment to walk and think while doing something else. It allowed me a moment to refocus and that, my friends, is priceless.

CHAPTER TWENTY
Testimonials From Real Humans

"My thoughts about the classroom, when after I started pedaling on the elliptical, it got me into a zone where I could focus more than anything. It also blocked out all distracting noise." ~ Finn T.

"The kinesthetic classroom was good to wake me up in the morning and get me ready for learning. It was also good to have breaks from learning by moving." ~ Jake

"I LOVED the run we did this morning, it really was fun and energizing." ~ Ben

"Moving helps me to get more fit. The cool part is it also calms me down when I am stressed." ~ Finn D.

Evan, a very sweet child with non-stop energy, reaffirmed why it is important to allow movement. His reasoning, "You are allowed to get rid of your energy, then you are ready for class."

Mia's mom told me, "She goes to sleep at night now at bedtime. I'm glad she can get a good night's sleep!"

Fourth grade teacher Amy Ryan commented, "I think for some students, it does help them. The students that need to be moving do seem to have fewer problems when they are on the bikes. However, we do a movement break in between every transition during the day. This allows for quite a bit of movement throughout the day. Sometimes active based learning takes place in their reading/ELA centers. For example, students may throw a ball back and forth or hula-hoop while defining words or discussing their book. Students are certainly more engaged during these activities and when they are using the bikes."

CHAPTER TWENTY-ONE
What Next?

Hopefully, you now know how to utilize these tables to maximize your students learning, but this really is a work in progress. There are so many things I am learning as I teach each day. I have barely had them two years and students help me discover more ways to help them learn by using the tables. I don't profess to know it all and am open to new suggestions. Feel free to contact me to let me know what you are doing, what works, what doesn't work, or just your opinion; I will be glad to include you as a resource.

Remember what I said in the beginning of this book, that you are a part of this too? Your part is this; spread the word about the importance of movement! It really is a no-brainer. We have to do this because there are many out there who have never heard of it or are scared of it. I believe fear is the biggest factor. Conversely, when students and adults alike come into my room for the first time, their faces light up. It is so neat to watch, and it is what every classroom should be like.

Wouldn't it be a wonderful thing to have students excited to move and running towards our classroom, instead of away from the classroom?

You have a part in this too. How will you make it happen? What changes will you implement first? Will you share it with your community? Will you contact your local news station and/or the newspaper too? What about utilizing social media and sharing it with loved ones who live far away? The more we talk, the less likely this is to go away. We need to let the students, parents, administration, and community members understand the importance of purposeful movement. It is not just another fad that will be forgotten, just as the last math or reading curriculum was.

By *Teaching Through Movement*, we become part of something bigger than our individual classrooms. We are fundamentally changing the way that students learn, and moving minds through purposeful movement in our kinesthetic classrooms.

Let's Keep in Touch!

I value your insight and ideas! Please feel free to contact me through one of these ways. Let's keep the dialogue going and learn from one another.

- Twitter: @StaceyShoecraft
- Facebook: www.facebook.com/stacey.shoecraft
- Website: http://staceyshoecraft.weebly.com/
- Edmodo: Mrs. Shoecraft. Contact me there and I will give you the code to join our group, "Learn2Move".

Acknowledgments

I dedicate *Teaching Through Movement* to all those who have brought me to this point:

- God for giving me the gift of teaching and the vision for the classroom I have today.
- Bob, always supportive and my rock.
- Bo and Jake, the two best boys a mommy could have. They taught me how to be a good teacher, from a kid's perspective.
- My principal, Leanne Sheppard, for her open-minded thinking and for financial support. My assistant principal, Tiffany Henderson, for taking me on a road trip to check out KidsFit on an October day.
- Lindsay Beck, the first person who opened up my mind to kinesthetic learning and for her introducing me to pivotal people. Thanks, Linds for all the equipment too!
- Ed Pinney, the director of KidsFit, who took a chance on me and helped us to build the first kinesthetic classroom in the country.
- Dave Spurlock for taking me under his wing, as he is a tireless advocate for kinesthetic learning.
- Jean Blaydes Moize, for teaching me her amazing ways and all things "Active Based Learning", she has changed learning for the better!
- Laura Bell Murphy and Michelle Anderson, my former team teaching pals. I could not do what I do without their support. They have put up with all

of the tours and last minute changes for filming. I am blessed beyond words to have worked with both of them!

- Sloane, Julia, Brooklyn, and Caroline and all of the former fifth grade students of mine. They helped the light bulb come on for me and began the movement that is sweeping across the nation. You really can learn from kids!

- Marie, my favorite Greek princess who sings Steve Miller better than Steve Miller. Oh yeah, and she cleaned up my writing to make me look "presentable".

- YOU, for caring enough to want to do something that will make such a positive impact. Thank you.

References

Fisher, Anne. <u>Fortune</u>. "Boys vs. Girls: What's Behind the College Grad Gender Gap?" 27 March 2013.

Hillman, Ph.D, Charles. "Overview of Naperville Central's Learning Readiness Physical Education Program."
Learning Readiness PE. 2008. Web 2013. <http://www.learningreadinesspe.com/overview. html>

Smail, Karen, Ph.D. The College of Charleston. Personal interview. 2015.

CPSIA information can be obtained
at www.ICGtesting.com
Printed in the USA
LVHW020008110619
620821LV00021B/791

9 780997 676174